GABRIEL
OF OUR LADY OF SORROWS

Gabriele Cingolani

Gabriel
OF OUR LADY OF SORROWS

Life and Prayers

Translated from the Italian by S.B. Zak

ALBA·HOUSE   NEW·YORK

SOCIETY OF ST. PAUL, 2187 VICTORY BLVD., STATEN ISLAND, NEW YORK 10314

ST PAULS

Italian language edition published by Editoriale ECO, s.r.l., San Gabriele (TE), Italy, under the title *Gabriele dell'Addolorata: Vita e preghiere.*
Scripture citations are taken from the New American Bible, copyright 1970 by the Confraternity of Christian Doctrine, Washington, D.C.; with revised New Testament, copyright 1986. All rights reserved. Used with permission.

Library of Congress Cataloging-in-Publication Data

Cingolani, Gabriele, 1940-
    [Gabriele dell'addolorata. English]
    Gabriel of Our Lady of Sorrows: life and prayers / Gabriele
Cingolani; translated from the Italian by S.B. Zak.
        p.   cm.
    ISBN 0-8189-0791-6
    1. Gabriel of Our Lady of Sorrows, Saint, 1838-1862. 2. Christian
saints — Italy — Biography. 3. Gabriel of Our Lady of Sorrows, Saint,
1838-1862 — Prayer-books and devotions — English.   I. Title.
BX4700.G2C5613   1997
282'.092 — dc21   97-8089
[B]   CIP

Produced and designed in the United States of America by the
Fathers and Brothers of the Society of St. Paul,
2187 Victory Boulevard, Staten Island, New York 10314,
as part of their communications apostolate.

ISBN: 0-8189-0791-6

Printing Information:

Current Printing - first digit   1   2   3   4   5   6   7   8   9   10

Year of Current Printing - first year shown

1997   1998   1999   2000   2001   2002   2003   2004   2005

Table of Contents

Triduum in the Form of a Liturgy of the Word

Biblical Abbreviations

OLD TESTAMENT

Genesis	Gn	Nehemiah	Ne	Baruch	Ba
Exodus	Ex	Tobit	Tb	Ezekiel	Ezk
Leviticus	Lv	Judith	Jdt	Daniel	Dn
Numbers	Nb	Esther	Est	Hosea	Ho
Deuteronomy	Dt	1 Maccabees	1 M	Joel	Jl
Joshua	Jos	2 Maccabees	2 M	Amos	Am
Judges	Jg	Job	Jb	Obadiah	Ob
Ruth	Rt	Psalms	Ps	Jonah	Jon
1 Samuel	1 S	Proverbs	Pr	Micah	Mi
2 Samuel	2 S	Ecclesiastes	Ec	Nahum	Na
1 Kings	1 K	Song of Songs	Sg	Habakkuk	Hab
2 Kings	2 K	Wisdom	Ws	Zephaniah	Zp
1 Chronicles	1 Ch	Sirach	Si	Haggai	Hg
2 Chronicles	2 Ch	Isaiah	Is	Malachi	Ml
Ezra	Ezr	Jeremiah	Jr	Zechariah	Zc
		Lamentations	Lm		

NEW TESTAMENT

Matthew	Mt	Ephesians	Eph	Hebrews	Heb
Mark	Mk	Philippians	Ph	James	Jm
Luke	Lk	Colossians	Col	1 Peter	1 P
John	Jn	1 Thessalonians	1 Th	2 Peter	2 P
Acts	Ac	2 Thessalonians	2 Th	1 John	1 Jn
Romans	Rm	1 Timothy	1 Tm	2 John	2 Jn
1 Corinthians	1 Cor	2 Timothy	2 Tm	3 John	3 Jn
2 Corinthians	2 Cor	Titus	Tt	Jude	Jude
Galatians	Gal	Philemon	Phm	Revelation	Rv

GABRIEL
OF OUR LADY OF SORROWS

A Life
that Soared to the
Heights

Soaring Like an Eagle

The following profile gives a quick introduction to Saint Gabriel of Our Lady of Sorrows.

To those who already know him, it is a chance to meet him anew, an opportunity to refresh their memory of him.

To those who do not yet know him, it gives an idea of who he was, serving as an invitation, if they so desire, to learn more about him from more detailed biographies.

This is not a complete and illustrated biography, but a short series of snapshots, a twelve-exposure roll as it were, focusing on his problems, the exuberance of his character, his choices, and above all his soul, which is much more difficult to get a picture of.

Gabriel is so alive that he could seem just like any other young person who is part of the crowd of boys and girls of today. He is the type of person you seem to meet at school, while out walking about on the streets, or out dancing at some discotheque. But then you realize that this Gabriel has disappeared, he has been carried away by values that we are barely able to make out.

It's not easy to understand him completely, but it's just about impossible not to like him. He is full of life, chases after happiness, has lots of problems but never gets lost; he meets challenges head-on and never gives up. He falls in love with everything that is good, but for a short period he does not succeed in putting everything in the proper perspective and isn't able to get his life in order. He races along the razor's edge and runs the risk of overlooking God's will for him. He just barely manages to pinpoint the right choice before it is too late.

He is not a convert who, realizing at a certain point that he has done everything wrong, changes the course of his life; rather he is a searcher who at a certain point finds what he has been looking for and gives himself to it completely with total commitment.

His soul soared like an eagle. It came to rest on a white summit, like the peak of the Gran Sasso, the massive rock formation in the mountainous Abruzzi region of Italy.

This summit was holiness.

It is good having a friend like him. He makes you realize that it is always possible to succeed; all you have to do is to have a sense of the good that is at work in all of us and then decide to put it into practice.

He reminds you that holiness means soaring to the heights — but starting off from situations just like ours. Just like his.

Welcome to the Gang

His was a family with a lot of pink and blue ribbons. The first of March, 1838, another little boy was born. They brought him that same day to be baptized at the Cathedral of Saint Rufinus, in the same baptistery where Saint Francis of Assisi was baptized, and they gave him the same name as that famous resident of Assisi, with the hope that it would bring him good things.

His father, Sante Possenti of Terni, was the papal governor of Assisi; his mother, Agnes Frisciotti of Civitanova in the Marches, was a housewife. They lived in the municipal building in the Town Square. Francis was the eleventh child, two of whom had already gone back to the Lord, and two more of whom would be born after him. The children, from oldest to youngest, were: Lawrence, Paul, Mary Louisa, Teresa, Lewis, Adele, Michael, Henry, Francis, Vincent and Rose.

The newborn took his place in the line of children and began the process of growing up without much ceremony. His coming into the world was a reason for celebration because he was another gift of life, but the Possenti household was already accustomed to such events. The excitement of the other children increased — who could touch him most, whom would he smile at first — but the worries of his mother and father also increased. It was too bad that shortly after his birth he had to be given to a wet nurse outside the home, since his mother Agnes, with all these children, did not have enough milk. But he was close by, in the village of Petrignano, and they could go see him whenever they wanted.

When he came back home, he was a beautiful bouncing baby boy by now a full year old. He was already able to recognize the others, and everyone was eager to cuddle him, to teach him to walk and to play. His voice was soon mixing with the others in claiming his own space, and his presence was unmistakable as the children would go tumbling down the stairs or as they ran through the courtyard. Frankie took advantage of the fact that the littlest ones were always able to get their way, and woe to those who tried to prevent him from getting what he wanted!

He had to learn right away that life was not all fun and games. His father would go off to the office, his mother would go shopping and take care of the house, his bigger brothers would go to school and when they were doing their homework he had to leave them in peace. Prayer also occupied an important place: there was the Sign of the Cross, the Hail Mary, the Our Father, the rosary. Especially in the evening, no one was allowed to sneak out of the house. When his mother or father made rules or gave explanations, no one was permitted to interrupt and everyone had to obey. Of course, his parents had to be patient if a yawn sometimes escaped from one of the little ones, or if they were overcome by sleep; but that was not to be the norm. In the Possenti home, life was taken seriously. Francis was part of all of this and did not put up a fuss, because that too was part of the game of life. His name was cut down to his size and became "Frankie," a nickname that the family would always use when referring to him.

Rough Weather Strengthens Roots

In his first four years so many changes occurred at home that Frankie could not figure things out. In 1839, his little brother Vincent was born, and it seemed that everyone's attention was given to him. In 1840, his father was named governor of Montalto in the Marches, and he went there without moving the whole family from Assisi, but taking only the six-year-old Michael and the ten-year-old Teresa with him; therefore, his father lived away from home and the family saw him only on holidays. For

Frankie, this period was filled with his mother Agnes. She looked after each child's maternal needs and also supplied the firmness of the fatherly role as well, though softening it at times. Frankie felt loved and protected. She gave him a sense of security and light-hearted fun; she had so many things that she had to do, but she seemed to be there only for him. He would be enchanted watching her doing everything that needed to be done while always seeming to have time for everyone, listening to her talk or sing, and especially finding her motionless in front of a little statue; he did not understand what she was doing, but they told him not to disturb her at those times because she was praying.

In 1841, his father Sante was promoted to the governorship of Poggio Mirteto in Lazio. The whole family packed up and moved to their new destination, but they were not happy there. The weather was humid, the house was small, his father became over-exhausted and had to leave the area in order to breathe some of the fresh air of his native Terni. Fortunately, this post did not last long. They remained there only from April to November, when they moved to Spoleto where Sante had been named legal assessor. There, the family set itself up in a nice big apartment with ten rooms, on the Via della Trattoria. But in the first few months after this move, one bad event took place after another, they came so quickly one after the other that they could not be stopped, kind of like the continuous passing of the landscape when you are travelling by train. While they were in Poggio Mirteto, the last pink ribbon had blossomed, Frankie's little sister who, appropriately enough, was named Rose. Frankie just barely made it in time to see her; she died on December 8, just six months old.

At the end of January of 1842, his nine-year-old sister Adele died suddenly of a cerebral hemorrhage. Shortly afterward his mother became seriously ill and everyone in the house was overcome with worry about the inevitable. Agnes herself realized that she was dying and wanted to hug and kiss her children, telling them that they would see each other again in Heaven. She gave Frankie a particularly tight hug and told him to be good and to keep praying. On February 9, 1842, she died with the same majestic dignity with which she had lived; she was forty-two years old. Frankie noticed that for a while, no one felt like laughing or playing any more. His father explained that their mother had left because she had been called by the "adorable will of God," and everyone tried to fill the empty space she had left as best they could. Frankie was not yet four years old.

Life Goes on, the Children Grow

With his schoolbag slung over his shoulder, Frankie began his elementary school studies in 1844 with the Brothers of the Christian Schools; classes were held in the Genga Building of Spoleto. He was now six years old and had grown well: he was a pleasant boy with a dark complexion, a slender build, quick reflexes, and strong muscles for running and going out on long walks. He had shown himself to be resilient after the loss of his mother. The family's governess, Pacifica Cucchi, and his sister Mary Louisa did everything they could to soften the blow; they lavished attention on him almost to the point of spoiling him.

In 1845, his sister Teresa came back home: she had left Assisi to accompany their father to Montalto and had remained in a school there in Cingoli. At fifteen years of age, she was now a young lady.

In 1846, Frankie received the Sacrament of Confirmation in the Church of Saint Gregory.

Two years passed. In 1848, Frankie noticed that his father wore a look of anguish on his face, like the one he had worn six years earlier: news had arrived that his brother Paul had died in Chioggia where he had gone to join the battle for the unification of Italy. The country was undergoing a period of turbulence during these years because of the desire for unity and democracy. The major events were the granting of democratic rights to the people, a Roman Republic, the Pope's exile to Gaeta and his return to Rome. But Frankie did not understand what any of this was about. To fill his world, all he needed were his friends from school and games, the homework he had to do, the prayers that he accepted without complaint, the company of his brothers and sisters, and the reassuring presence of his father Sante. He got along with everybody. He felt loved, and he also knew how to win people's affection. He was obedient and loving, notwithstanding some mischief.

His father was an inspiration to him; only rarely was his discipline heavy. He experienced him as strong but gentle, demanding but understanding. His father was honest in his official duties and would not accept bribes. He was generous with the poor. Frankie would see him pray for long periods in the morning before he went off to work; he was attentive to him in the evenings when he led the family rosary and gave instructions regarding family duties. He felt that his father was securely in control of the family.

In 1850, Frankie enrolled in the faculty of humanities, more or less like a middle school and high school with an emphasis on classical studies, conducted by the Jesuits in Spoleto. There he made his First Holy Communion, probably on June 21, 1851, the feast of Saint Aloysius Gonzaga. The six intense years he spent with the Jesuits at this school were a determining factor in the development of his personality.

He enjoyed the academic work and did well in his studies. He was a source of satisfaction to his professors and a model that his classmates sought to imitate. He felt deeply fulfilled with his life. As he learned the literary, scientific and philosophical material that was little by little becoming a part of him in his classical studies, he strengthened his inner sense of security and mastery over the future.

The results of his work were not late in coming and fully repaid him for his effort: he was awarded first and second prizes practically every year. In many subjects he was given honorable mention. He earned the gold medal in philosophy, and if he did not do much better than average in mathematics, oh well. There was a slight drop in his academic performance in 1852; this was due to the changes brought on by puberty, which made him spend entire days without the least desire to do anything or with unbridled eagerness to play and enjoy himself. Despite this, as a whole, that year went well enough anyway.

In 1853, some changes in the family made him stop and think more than usual. In February, the news of his brother Lawrence's death arrived from Rome; later reports explained that he had taken his own life as a consequence of some Masonic connections. In September, his sister Teresa married the lawyer Pellegrino Pellegrini in the parish church of Saint Ansano. His brother Lewis, who was already a member of the Dominicans, moved from Perugia to Lucca where he would prepare for the priesthood.

Frankie was fifteen years old, and his desire to live life to the full overcame whatever difficulties these turns of events might have had on him. His life was full: he made a good impression at school, was successful in society, was held in high esteem by his peers, and built good strong friendships. He would organize hunting expeditions, which was the favorite sport among the boys in his day, and he enjoyed taking part in walks and excursions into the country. He willingly went with his father or sisters and family friends to the theater, joined in friendly card games, attended dances, engaged in intelligent and refined conversation, read Manzoni, Grossi, Tommaseo and Bresciani. And he was frequently featured on stage, giving some recitation or other at school assemblies where he would be showered with applause. Not bad, even if these worldly pleasures would sometimes desensitize his spiritual awareness or muddle his thoughts when he went to pray.

Time to Fall in Love

What would he do as a grown-up? Everyone asked the question. Different people would put together various scenarios for him, starting with his father and some of the girls who would come by to visit the family. He himself was head over heels in love with life. You could tell that by how he gave himself so completely to whatever he was doing; but he was still undecided about the future. There was an old idea that still attracted him at least as much as school success and romantic friendships did: the idea of joining himself to God and serving others in the Religious life. He had even promised to do so a couple of times when he got such a bad sore throat that he thought he would die of suffocation. As a matter of fact, the second time this happened he was certain that he was saved from his illness by a miracle, and afterward he actually did make a formal request to join the Jesuits, but nothing ever came of it.

Every once in a while something would make him stop and think that this life, even if it was so beautiful, was held in place only by a tiny thread; the littlest thing was enough to make it end without your even realizing it. How could he not think in terms like this with all the deaths that had occurred in his family and having already run the risk of dying himself? He remembered also the time he had gone off hunting with his brothers; they made him carry the rifle, even though he was only a minor, and as he was jumping over a little brook, the rifle went off: he just missed blowing his own brains out! The sound of the rifle shot still rang in his ears. These were thoughts that could have been forgotten, but they were always there and they would always come to mind when he was faced with important decisions.

Frankie was able to put the decision off without too much difficulty, however; after all, for the time being there were plenty of things to do if he was to prepare himself for life. He had to finish school; he had to help his father in the office where he too worked as personal secretary ever since his brother Michael had gone off to the University in Rome. His father himself would encourage him to take his time whenever he mentioned the idea of joining some Religious Order.

Meanwhile, he was not only a devout Catholic who practiced his faith, but he was also selfless and generous. He would always find something to give to the poor; he would help his classmates who did not do so well in school; he would be the first to stretch out his hand if someone in the family needed some help. He would engage in many enjoyable activities, and with a real passion, but never anything indecent or immoral. An acquaintance of his found this out when he went up to him and made a lewd suggestion: Frankie chased after him with a pruning knife until this other fellow, out of fear, had run a safe distance away.

However, Frankie was now seventeen years old and he had to make a decision one way or the other; otherwise he really would fall in love and the decision would be made for him. In the winter of 1854 - 1855, other people noticed that Mary Pennacchietti, the daughter of a lawyer friend of the Possenti's, had a crush on him. For his part, he liked her too and was very nice to her. They would exchange novels and, with the involvement of Frankie's sister Teresa, they met at the opera to see "Il Trovatore."

At the same time, Frankie was becoming ever more dashing in his manner of dressing and more and more refined in the dance halls and in social conversations. He was a good-looking guy and he knew it. He was tall and slender with a dark complexion; his face was round and gentle with piercing dark eyes, delicately shaped lips that were always smiling, and dark brown hair with unruly waves. When he would dress in the manner of the day, he seemed to wear the latest style triumphantly. He was known as the "fashion plate" or the fancy dancer. His father was quite content with all this, happy that Frankie was fitting so well into society. And the thought that Frankie's attraction to Religious life had disappeared into blessed oblivion made him smile. In this phase of being drunk with life, Frankie lived in a semi-dazed state. Without consciously telling himself so, he realized that his life.was drifting along on its own, being caught up in the current, following the flow that everyone else was taking. For him it was a great life.

In the summer of 1855, the magic disappeared once more. His sister Mary Louisa died suddenly while he was at the Corpus Christi procession. This did not seem possible: she was only twenty-six years old, a blossoming young woman who for him was part mother, part sister, and always his friend in the ups and downs of life.

There followed a difficult year in which he was not able to make any decision. He got involved in his studies as usual and took part in social activities, but without the carefree attitude that he had had before. He would go to the theater but disappeared before the show was over in order to go pray at the Cathedral; he would dress in a stylish manner and go to dances but beneath his finery he wore a hair shirt that would scratch his skin. His father would suggest different activities that were intended to distract him from his interest in Religious life, and he would always agree to participate in them but never whole-heartedly. He did what he was supposed to do but he was not happy and inside he was distancing himself from these things. Something else still needed to happen to make him decide once and for all.

On August 22, the octave of the feast of the Blessed Virgin Mary's Assumption, there was a great feastday in Spoleto. The townspeople all gathered to honor the ancient Eastern image of Our Lady that was kept in the Cathedral; through her intercession the city had been freed from many dangers. During the 1856 celebration, Frankie was a part of the crowd; he was a bit distracted and felt self-conscious inside because he was not sure what to do. The image of Our Lady was being carried in procession by the Bishop. When it passed by him, he sensed that Our Lady's eyes in the image became alive and looked directly at him, into his innermost being. And with this sensation of being stared at, there was a voice: Francis, what are you doing? Don't you see that this life is not made for you? Become a Religious.

It was done. Neither death nor fear had

ever made him give in completely. What had been needed was an invitation of limitless love. Frankie had always been devoted to Our Lady. He had learned this devotion from his mother. It was confirmed in the example he got from his father, and it continued to grow in the religious training he received at the Sodality of Mary that was connected with the Jesuit school in Spoleto. But this time it hit him like a bolt of lightning. She had struck him with her resolute glance, and from that moment on he was madly and irreversibly in love. No one could stop him any longer. This took place on August 22, and on September 9 he was already in the novitiate with the Passionists at Morrovalle in the Marches.

His father no longer recognized him. He had made his decision and there was no making him change his mind. He did not even stop to consider his father's latest invitation to think about what he was doing and to wait a bit. The evening of September 5, he took part in the recitation that had already been scheduled for the close of the academic year. He showed up dressed in the latest style "from overseas and beyond the mountains," and brought on a storm of applause. Both his father and the Bishop were moved by his performance. The morning of the 6th, very early, he left for the novitiate, removing himself from the worldliness of

Spoleto that had enticed him so with dreams and hopes. The Possenti and Pennacchietti families had planned a party, or had set a trap in the guise of a party, for that evening, hoping that it would lead to an official engagement announcement; but it was all in vain.

The evening of September 7, Frankie was in Loreto. The 8th was the feast of Our Lady's birth and Frankie spent the entire day in the Holy House. It was at this time that he made with Our Lady his new and unchangeable pact of love. On the 9th, he arrived at his destination. While he was making this trip, two of his relatives who were priests, one in Loreto and the other in Morrovalle, tried to dissuade him from the decision he had made, but it was a waste of time. Only when the door to the Passionist House closed behind him and the Passionist community celebrated with him as with a newly arrived brother, only then did he feel safe and begin to smile once more.

In the Right Place

From this moment on, his life really soared to the heights. He remained in Morrovalle until June of 1858. He completed the novitiate and stayed on another nine months to perfect his

Latin and philosophy, which was necessary if he was to become a priest.

In taking on the Passionist habit, he also changed his name: he was no longer called Francis Possenti, but Gabriel of Our Lady of Sorrows. This change of name made it clear that his past was definitively behind him. The period of his novitiate gave him time to learn about the family he had chosen for himself: the Rule of the community, the history, daily schedules, traditions, the purpose of their life as Passionists, their spirituality, mission, and important members of the Passionist family. He gave himself to this new task of learning with all the commitment that he had demonstrated up to that point in time, the same commitment that had always allowed him to get everything out of life that could possibly be gotten out of it.

In some things he already seemed like an expert, in others he would become so after just a few months. He knew how to pray like one who already had much experience, so much so that when he would report to the novice master about his prayer, an elderly Religious stopped at the door to eavesdrop.

The Crucified Lord and Our Lady of Sorrows were the backbone of the Passionist life, and he knew them better than the other novices because ever since he was a little boy he had contemplated them in the statue of the Pietà which had been the heart of the Possenti home. He felt an inner peace and joy that he had never succeeded in attaining before, regardless of how much he had run after them. He wrote this in a letter to his father, and also tried in this way to reassure him: "My life inside here is bursting with joy."

On September 22, 1857, he finished the novitiate. He bound himself to God with the vows to focus his life on Christ's Passion and to be poor, chaste and obedient. He gave himself to these vows with such determination that even the oldest members of the community were impressed. In this new life of his, he did not need to warm himself up or train himself, but he took off immediately at top speed.

When there arrived the news that a twenty-four-year-old student had died in another Passionist House, he experienced a throb of envy and asked for the grace to die young himself so that his sacrifice would be all the more fresh and new. His director, Father Norbert, who took the place of the novice master Father Raphael, did not find out about this request of Gabriel's in time to forbid him from making it, and his reprimand did not annul the request that had been made.

While he was still in Morrovalle, he made a trip to Fermo to see his sister Teresa and take care of some family business that had to be notarized. She hardly recognized him in his new get-up: the habit, his very short haircut, his eyes kept low. But she was struck by his new interior maturity.

On June 20, 1858, he was transferred to Pievetorina, a tiny little town in the Apennines of the Marches region. There he completed rounding out his study of Thomistic philosophy and began the regular course work in theology. Over the winter, he became ill once more with the infection that he already knew so well; it caused his throat to swell and made breathing difficult. But the prospect of death no longer frightened him because he was given over to the love of God and to his will.

In the spring, the Possenti governess Pacifica came to visit from not-so-far-away Spoleto. She had always felt that Frankie was also a bit her own son, and she arrived all overjoyed and making a fuss, telling him how he should eat and dress. When she saw him, however, the words just died on her lips and the hug that she was already directing toward him just kind of froze: this was not the Frankie she had known. Gabriel assured her that he was well and happy, and he reminded her to be faithful to prayer and in helping the poor.

His brother Michael, now a medical student in Rome, also came to visit him and remained a few days with him. Thinking that he looked weak, he tried to ask him if it would not have been better to return home. Gabriel explained that such a notion was absurd. He felt as though his whole being were rejoicing. He had found what he had always been looking for, and no one had suspected that it was right here all the time. This was the greatest grace imaginable, it could not be thrown away. While they were talking about these things and walking about the garden, he stopped to pick a daisy from the flower bed that he tended so that Our Lady's altar would have flowers, and he offered it to Michael, as if to say that he understood, that he loved him, but there could be no compromise on how to live one's life: for him the problem had been resolved. Then he realized that he had picked the flower without having asked permission and he threw himself on his knees before the Superior and begged for forgiveness.

In Pievetorina, some boys who would come to the Passionist house for private lessons noticed that at the time set aside for the Passionists to go for a walk, Gabriel would disappear down the path that led to the stream. So one day they hid themselves in the brush and found him in prayer, kneeling on the rocks, with his arms outstretched as if in ecstasy, in front of a picture of Our Lady.

Time for Growing Up

He remained in Pievetorina just a year. On July 4, 1859, he left for Abruzzi. After a stop at the Passionist House in Recanati and another visit to Our Lady of Loreto, the group of students crossed the border into the Papal State, then entered the Kingdom of Naples, and finally arrived on July 10 at their new destination: Isola del Gran Sasso in the province of Teramo.

In this new location, Gabriel continued his theology studies, received the ministries of minor orders and prepared himself for the priesthood. Above all, he continued his efforts to become holy; he proceeded with the velocity of a cruise ship that was travelling at top speed and that never slowed down even for a moment.

His studies posed no problem for him. The subject matter consisted of theology, biblical studies, and liturgy; things that not only enlighten the mind but fill the heart and are an aid to prayer. He undertook these studies so that he could become a priest and missionary, and he was so desirous of attaining this goal that he did not waste any time at all. While he was with his books, his thoughts were crowded with the throngs that were waiting to receive instruction and hear the proclamation that brought salvation.

He got along well in the community. Coming from a big family and being surrounded always by many friends, he understood the problems that could arise in groups and the need to be flexible. Here, the camaraderie that was shared was something different. They did not talk about unimportant things but about what they were studying in school and what they felt in their hearts when they were at prayer. Gabriel had become famous for his ability to speak about Our Lady in a way that almost seemed to cast a spell over the listeners. If he was given the chance to speak on this topic, he took off like a skyrocket, and he would not stop. His companions did not know where all these thoughts came from. They had never seen anyone so in love with Our Lady. He was a mixture of love or a blazing fire of love, his director used to say. His love was so full that it could not be contained.

Our Lady was a permanent presence in his heart. He had fallen in love so completely that there was no room for even the slightest errant thought. For her, he could do anything and refuse nothing; he was able to overcome any difficulty and abandon himself completely in trust. He would go around kissing her image wherever he found it, he would send her greetings at every opportunity, he wanted to wake up every quarter hour even during the night so that he could think of her.

Whatever he did seemed too little, so he came up with some bizarre ideas. He wanted her name burnt onto his chest with a red-hot branding iron, or at least etched there with a penknife; he wanted to take a vow promising to speak of her when he was a missionary; he composed a list of praises to Mary that he called his Marian Creed, and he wanted to recopy it in blood, or at least sign it in blood. But he never got the chance to actually do any of these strange things because he was never given permission, and so he had to be content with just the desire to do them. Once, when he was speaking about Our Lady, a confrere saw a flame leap from Gabriel's heart, and this confrere felt that he too was then flooded with love for Our Lady, a love that remained with him for the rest of his life.

For Gabriel, the Blessed Virgin was above all Our Lady of Sorrows, as he had learned when he was a little boy. He restored a statue that had been abandoned in the attic of the Passionist House and put it back in use for veneration. When he meditated on her sorrows, he felt that he was already in Heaven because he would discover the greatest possible love. She revealed to him the mystery of the Crucified Lord, which is the focal point of the Passionist vocation. It was through her eyes that he loved and contemplated this mystery. With her in-

27

struction, he transformed himself into a little version of the Crucified One.

He would also speak about the Crucified Lord and about Our Lady of Sorrows to the people he would meet when he went out to get fresh air; he would talk about them especially to young people. In this way, young people came to know him and referred to him as the one who walked around in a recollected state and who spoke about Our Lady.

The strong point of his life, and the thing that he liked most when he joined the Passionists, was prayer. He wrote to his father that a quarter hour in church with the doors closed (the Passionists would close them in order to avoid distractions) was worth more than all the pleasures that the world could offer. He immersed himself so completely in the heart of the Crucified Lord and of Our Lady of Sorrows that he seemed almost to be one with them; but he was not able to keep this fullness of love inside, and sighs and tears would sometimes come upon him, embarrassing him in the presence of others. At Mass, he was like a statue; when receiving Holy Communion, like an angel. The people already referred to him as the saintly little Brother.

The yearning to share the same feelings that were those of the Crucified Lord and Our Lady of Sorrows made him wish to make every possible sacrifice and recite all the prayers that he could. He wanted to be a part of all the good that existed and of all the love that was given. His director was not able to get him to go easy with these things. Because he wanted to become a martyr, he greatly increased the personal sacrifices he would make. He found ways of making sacrifices in eating, drinking, standing, walking, when he was at school, in his room and at recreation; he made all these sacrifices not to destroy himself but to make himself more amenable to the will of God. His love was impatient and God would sometimes draw him to himself in ways that did not always seem opportune.

He had taken to practicing so many devotions that he had to finish them at night by candle light. However, he was not satisfied with all that he was doing and would burst into tears at the thought that he was not able to attain the level of holiness that corresponded to the desire that God had put inside him. He called his director into his room and fell on his knees before him imploring: please, tell me if there is anything in my heart that is displeasing to God, because I want to tear it out! His director assured him that he was doing well. Later on the director will testify that he never saw in him a consciously committed venial sin.

Time for Finishing the Work Begun

If even a person with great stamina would be exhausted by keeping up such a pace, imagine Gabriel whose physical state was always delicate.

At the end of 1861, his chest pains had returned and breathing became difficult. It seemed to be his usual illness, instead it was tuberculosis. Tuberculosis in those days was what cancer is for us today. He had completed his preparations for priesthood, but political difficulties prevented any ordinations from taking place.

Gabriel realized that nothing could be done. He had arrived at the end of the road and was now on the threshold of what lay beyond. But he was not upset. This was precisely what he had asked for a few years earlier, during his first experience of that love which satisfied every longing. Now, he was so completely immersed in that love that living in it here or living in it there made little difference. It would have been nice to have taken another step and to have seen his dream of being a priest become reality, but what did that really matter? The only thing that really mattered was the will of God. "This is what God wants, this is what I want too," he wrote.

The morning of February 27, 1862, as the

first light of dawn shone on the face of Gran Sasso, Gabriel was in bed in his room, surrounded by the community; they had been summoned by the bell as it tolled an impending death. He said his good-byes to all of them, promised to remember them in Paradise, and asked for their forgiveness and prayers. Then, sensing that he had no more breath and that his heart was stopping, he gave himself over to the love that had taken possession of these last six years of his life, and said: "Mary, dear Mother of mine, come fast." And then he smiled toward the wall where he saw her coming to welcome him to his new home. Even in death he gave expression to his unrestrainable desire to live. He breathed no more. Only his smile remained.

* * * * *

This is the first part of his story. The second part starts at this point, and it is still going on today under the eyes of everyone and can be recounted by anyone who is devoted to him.

It burst into full bloom thirty years after his death, in 1892, when thousands of people living in Abruzzi flocked to his tomb when his body was exhumed and he made his presence felt by sending a shower of miracles. It continued in 1908 with his beatification and in 1920 with his canonization. The story was spread with the construction of the first shrine; with the magazine *The Echo of Saint Gabriel* — which today has more than half a million readers; with the construction of the second shrine — because the first was no longer large enough to accommodate the millions of pilgrims who came to visit it from every part of the world.

Everyone is drawn to him because everyone finds him attractive. He embodies the values that we are seeking even today: the desire to live, to succeed, to find fulfillment, and to be happy; the capacity to obey, but also the longing to be free and the refusal to be manipulated; an appreciation of life and of everything beautiful that life offers.

The sick are drawn to him because his health was always fragile, but that did not decrease his passion for living.

Students are drawn to him because he was always a student, and in his studies he learned new reasons to love life.

Those who are disappointed and misunderstood are drawn to him because he was not overwhelmed by the difficulties he faced, he always bounced back and knew how to find what he needed in order to be happy and to love what life brought him.

Young people especially are drawn to him because when all is said and done, his story is none other than that of falling in love: falling in love with family, with school, with having a good time, with friends, with success; until he felt the loving gaze of Our Lady who won him over by revealing to him the Crucified Lord and the giving of himself as the one complete response. From that point on he was an incandescent flame.

Prayers
to Saint Gabriel

Liturgical Prayers

O God,
according to your marvelous plan of love
you called Saint Gabriel
of Our Lady of Sorrows
to live the mystery of the Cross
together with Mary, the Mother of Jesus;
guide our spirit
to your Crucified Son
so that as sharers
in his Passion and Death
we may obtain the glory of the Resurrection.
We ask this through Christ our Lord. Amen.

* * * * *

O Lord,
you taught Saint Gabriel
of Our Lady of Sorrows
to meditate assiduously
on the sorrows of your dearest Mother,
and by means of her
you raised him
to the greatest heights of holiness;
grant that we,
by his intercession and example,
may live so closely united
to your Sorrowful Mother
that we will always enjoy
her maternal protection.

You who are God, and live and reign
with the Father and the Holy Spirit,
one God for ever and ever. Amen.

* * * * *

O God,
you marked the soul
of Saint Gabriel of Our Lady of Sorrows
profoundly with the imprint
of the sufferings of Christ your Son
and with the sorrows of the Blessed Virgin,
        his Mother;
grant that we,
living as he did
with our spirit turned towards
the mystery of our salvation,
may make joyful and quick progress
on the way of perfection.
We ask this through our Lord Jesus Christ,
        your Son,
who lives and reigns with you and the Holy
        Spirit,
one God, for ever and ever. Amen.

A Prayer
For Patronal Feasts

Saint Gabriel of Our Lady of Sorrows, loving Saint of the smile, we seek your intercession that we may receive God's blessings on our lives and on all of humanity.

You see the level of mastery that humankind has risen to through the use of the gifts of creation. But at the same time humanity has not been able to overcome the shameful situations of sin, such as injustice, misunderstandings between people and nations, pollution, violence and drug abuse. May all people receive the light of the Holy Spirit in order to understand and respect God's plan in creation and in the relationships between human beings.

Heedful always of the interior voice of grace, you lived in the midst of the world without being overcome by temptation and without compromising your integrity. Accepting your personal call to perfection, you found the meaning and fulfillment of life in the love of Christ Crucified and of Our Lady of Sorrows. Intercede for us with our heavenly Mother and her Crucified Son, that we may receive the grace to hold fast to the will of God in all that he asks of us every day in our particular state of life.

Teach us to spend our lives in the service of others, because this is the will of the Father and this is how the Kingdom of God will grow in our world.

Let us live the Christian life consistently, with sensitivity to the needs of the poor, and the ability to fight for justice and the personal dignity of others; make us credible witnesses of the Baptism we have received and of the Eucharist that we celebrate every week.

Grant your protection to families: to parents when they are fearful, to the children as they grow, to adolescents and young adults in their hopes and aspirations, to the elderly in their loneliness. Grant that everyone will live their own state in life as a personal vocation and mission.

Help us to understand that suffering is part of our life and that through suffering life is made more precious, because it makes us sharers in the Passion of Jesus. Grant that we may commit ourselves to the values of this life without forgetting that God is the ultimate good and the final destiny of our existence.

By means of your intercession, may our Heavenly Father grant us forgiveness for our sins and perseverance in doing good. Amen.

A Pilgrim's Prayer

I thank you, Saint Gabriel, for satisfying my desire to come to your shrine and pray at your tomb, where your smile greets those who are devoted to you.

With myself I bring my deepest desires, the fatigue of the road travelled, the failures and the joys of my life, and above all the confidence that you can obtain for me the graces that I need.

An encounter with you is always an experience that renews me. This pilgrimage, which I feel the need to repeat every so often, is an important stage in the greater pilgrimage that I am making toward our eternal home. Help me to draw from this experience all the good that I possibly can for my growth as a Christian.

Guide me to an encounter with God that will purify and confirm my faith. Bring me to Jesus the Crucified Lord so that he may forgive my sins and strengthen my will to be a better person. Help me to make a good confession and to participate worthily in the community celebration of the Eucharist.

Ask Our Sorrowful Mother, to whom you were so devoted, to grant me her protection, so that I may respond to my vocation as you did to yours. Grant that after this visit to your shrine I will be more constant in living the Christian life, in participating in the life of my parish, and in setting a good example for everyone.

Besides these most important graces, I beseech you, dear Saint Gabriel, to intercede for me that the Lord may grant me the assistance that I feel particularly in need of at this time, and that I ask for in a special way during this pilgrimage: (*here, mention your particular requests concerning health, work, family, school, choices to be made, people who are dear to you, the deceased, etc.*).

Through your intercession, may I discover the will of God every day and accept and love the people with whom I live and the events that take place around me.

May your example give me the strength and steadfastness to live as a true Christian despite the difficulties of this period of history. Grant that my efforts to obtain material well-being will not cause me to neglect the more important values of life, such as friendship, solidarity, caring for those who suffer, holding fast to Christ and his Church.

As I am making my way back home, let your smile and serenity remain in my heart, for these are the essence of your teaching and intercession. Grant that I may make your smile my own, as an expression of love for life, giving it to the brothers and sisters I meet, giving it to God himself.

Thank you and good-bye for now, dear Saint Gabriel.

Children's Prayer

Dear Saint Gabriel, hear the prayer that we confidently place before you. Obtain for us the grace to grow like Jesus and to love Jesus above all things. Help us to listen to what our parents and teachers tell us, and to follow the voice that the Lord has put in our hearts.

You know how much we like to play. In our games, help us to understand each other and to cooperate with each other; help us not to hurt the feelings of others and to avoid saying bad words. Let there be no bad children among us, but only good children who are respectful. Teach us to enjoy school, to do our homework with diligence, to be faithful in our catechism lessons and in prayer, and to be loyal in relationships among ourselves and with grownups.

You were devoted to Our Blessed Mother, obtain her motherly protection for us. You were strong before God because you always loved him, help us to do his will every day. Amen.

A Young Person's Prayer

Dear Saint Gabriel, in this period of my life I am particularly in need of help. Obtain for me from the Lord the light to understand his plan in my regard and the strength to carry it out faithfully.

I feel the need to be free. Help me to use my freedom with respect for the freedom of others. Teach me to use my freedom to make proper choices, that is, by giving myself to others and not taking advantage of them.

I feel the need to love and to be loved. Help me to perceive my vocation and to respond to it generously. Make me aware of the problems of others, especially my own parents and those who are close to me.

Help me to be able to accept my responsibilities in my family, in my parish and in society, and to fulfill them with honesty, bearing positive witness to Christ as my Baptism requires.

You who loved life and discovered its fullness in love for the Crucified Lord and for Our Lady of Sorrows, help me to understand that every human value finds its fulfillment in God. Amen.

A Student's Prayer

Dear Saint Gabriel, I entrust my studies to your protection; at this time, they are my most important responsibility.

You were a student your whole life and it

was as a student that you attained great holiness.

In your studies, you always discovered new reasons to love life, first as you were drawn to success in society, then as you moved toward the goal of priesthood. Help me to understand that school is indispensable for building my personality and for my future success.

Help me always to discover the wisdom of God and the greatness of humanity in my studies; help me to learn to admire creation and the conquests of science; help me to understand my vocation so that I will find the proper way in which I am called to serve others.

Help me so that my efforts in preparing for exams and for entering the professional world of work will be crowned with success.

Help me to make my studies a way to love those people who have placed their trust in me and those whom God will put into my life in the future. Let my studying be a preparation not only for earning a living for myself and those who are dear to me, but above all let it be a preparation for making my life a gift to others in the Christian community and in society. Amen.

A Prayer For Those Involved in Sports

Dear Saint Gabriel, we entrust to your protection our sports activities.

Your life was a race where you always came in first, a match that you won in every aspect. In the first phase, as a lay person in the world, you crossed the finish line of goodness and generosity; you were the best in school, in fostering harmony in the family, and in faithfulness to your Christian duties. In the second phase, as a member of the Passionist community, you won the greatest Christian victory: holiness.

Following your example, we do not want the commitment that we show in preparing for different sporting events to be limited only to the sports contests we engage in, but we want that same commitment to permeate our whole lives.

In our competition, help us to build friendships and team spirit, to be loyal and selfless, to bear witness to all the other values that make living in human society pleasant: good competition, fraternity, cooperation, respect, non-violence.

In our victories, help us not to be proud but to share our joy with others. In our losses help us to recognize the merit of the others and not to feel downcast but spurred on to do better.

Above all, obtain for us from Jesus the Crucified Lord and from Mary his Sorrowful Mother the grace to not fall short of life's final goal: eternal salvation. Amen.

A Prayer For Engaged Couples

Dear Saint Gabriel, we feel the need to entrust to your protection the joy and delight of our love, because you understand us and can obtain for us from God the graces that we need in this important period of our developing maturity.

Our love is a great gift that has been given over to our responsibility. Help us to live it according to the plan of God, because only in doing his will shall we be able to find fulfillment.

We need to understand each other and to accept each other, to respect the gifts that God has given to each of us and to prepare ourselves in freedom to give ourselves as a gift to the other. We know that this is a difficult road, laden with the hidden snares of selfishness and weakness. Help us not to be blinded by the superficial aspects of our relationship but to build it faithfully to full maturity.

Let the communion that is experienced between us be an incentive to engage in work with others and for others, in our families, in the parish, in our places of employment, and among those in society who are most in need.

Help us to understand the gift and the mission of Christian married life, which means not only loving each other in truth, but being a sign of the love between Christ and the Church. May our engagement prepare us to bear witness to the richness of the sacrament that we will receive through the "yes" we will pronounce at the altar. Amen.

A Prayer For Spouses

Dear Saint Gabriel, we ask you to place our family under your protection and to help us to raise our family according to the plan of God. Let the grace of the sacrament of marriage that we have received strengthen our love day after day so that we may bear witness to God's love in the midst of the community of men and women.

Enlighten our consciences so that we may properly fulfill our responsibilities as mother and father. Let our love be at the service of life in welcoming children and in coming to the assistance of the weak, the poor, and the abandoned of society.

Obtain for us the grace to know how to talk to our children and to understand their problems. Help us to realize that our children are not our property but that they belong to God who has called them to life through us; he entrusts to each one of them a mission and we must place ourselves at the service of that mission.

Let our family know peace, harmony, love, and good health; let the trials of life not discourage us, but may they help us to understand better the love of God and his will for us. Amen.

A Worker's Prayer

Dear Saint Gabriel, I turn to you to ask for your protection in my life as a worker.

Through you, I wish to thank the Lord for my job; for it allows me to live a serene life with my family.

In the work-place, help me to do my job every day with the attitude of one who cooperates with God's own work of creation and let me offer my life in service to others.

My work calls me to make new things with the material God has created. My activity is, in turn, the creation of new products that are useful for society. I pass my days with machinery and in hard work, and in this way my life is spent and used. Help me to live this job as my vocation and, in union with Jesus the Crucified Lord, as my way of loving and giving my life for those whom I love and for the brothers and sisters who will benefit from the fruits of my labor.

Protect me from accidents. Let me be an instrument of justice and peace in the workplace.

Help the unemployed to find a job and inspire community leaders to provide for a just and equitable distribution of goods.

In my work, help me to respond to God's plan for me and to find my fulfillment in Christ. Amen.

A Sick Person's Prayer

Dear Saint Gabriel, I turn to you trusting that through your intercession I will receive from God the grace and strength that I need.

Help me to accept my situation with faith and to consider my sickness not as a misfortune, but as an invitation to understand better the meaning and purpose of life. Strengthen my faith so that I will be able to see my pain as a precious gift and an occasion to love more.

In your own illness, as a small boy, you prayed with faith and received the grace of being healed. Later, seriously ill at the height of your youth, you accepted God's will with unbounded love.

Obtain for me from God the grace to be healed if it is his will, so that I can dedicate myself to the service of others with new strength and love.

Obtain for me above all the grace to accept my illness, for however long it may last, as God's plan to unite me to the Passion of Christ, completing it in his Body, which is the Church, for the salvation of the world. Amen.

A Prayer For the Elderly

O glorious Saint Gabriel, receive into your protecting embrace our lives that have now reached maturity and are ready to have their fruits harvested.

Obtain for us from the Lord the grace to accept our situation with joy and to place it at the service of the younger generation with the good example of a smile, of equilibrium, and of availability with discrete advice and active silence.

Enlighten the leaders of society so that

they will not evaluate people only in terms of what they can produce, but according to the value of life itself. Do not let us consider illness and old age as useless time, but as precious time that enables us to attain maturity of spirit and wisdom of life.

As our physical strength diminishes, let our faith grow stronger and our capacity to love increase, so that we will be ready to enter into the full vision of God. Do not let us lose esteem and love for this life as we start on the way to fullness of life. Amen.

A Prayer For Vocations

Dear Saint Gabriel, we turn to your intercession so that we may obtain the grace to live the vocation we received in Baptism.

Help us to hear, among the many voices that reach us, the personal call of the Lord, and let us follow his voice for the rest of our lives.

We praise God for the generosity with which you responded to your vocation to become a Passionist, despite the difficulties posed by your pleasure-seeking youth. Help us, too, to follow the impulse of grace in choosing the direction for our lives before it is too late.

If we are called to married and family life

in the sacrament of matrimony, help us to understand the responsibility and commitment of that life, and help us to prepare ourselves to take our places in society as witnesses of the love of God who is Creator and Redeemer.

To those who feel called to serve the community through the ministry of priesthood, grant the generosity that is needed to overcome uncertainty and to give themselves to working full-time for the sanctification of God's people.

If it is the will of God that some of us should be consecrated to him in a special way through the Religious life, obtain for us the wisdom to understand with insight, and the courage to respond with generosity.

With your example and your intercession, let new brothers and sisters gladden your Passionist family, to announce to the world the love of the Crucified Lord and of Our Lady of Sorrows, the love that inflamed and consumed your own youth.

We ask you to intercede with the Lord so that the Church of our day will slacken neither the witness it bears through the radical living of the evangelical counsels, nor its proclamation that God alone is the absolute good and the final destiny of humanity. Amen.

A Prayer For the Blessing of Vehicles

Our help is in the name of the Lord.
Who made heaven and earth.

The Lord be with you.
And also with you.

Let us pray: O Lord, you who sustain, move and govern all things with your all-powerful goodness: guide our lives, we beseech you, and be with us in our travels. Make us careful, for ourselves and for others, and help us to use our vehicles without causing harm to anyone, keeping us always under the protection of our guardian angels.

Bless us and this vehicle. Free us from the dangers of the road and preserve our lives for your glory, so that we may work for good and come to merit everlasting happiness.

Saint Gabriel, our holy patron, be with us in a special way when we use this vehicle for work and for moving about; may we know how to use it always for our good and for the good of others. Amen.

TRIDUUM
To Request a Special Grace

The following formula can be used when one wishes to turn in a special way to the intercession of Saint Gabriel:
> — *in time of illness;*
> — *when exams are drawing near;*
> — *to prepare oneself for important decisions;*
> — *when loved ones are in need;*
> — *etc.*

I. O Saint Gabriel, you sought God's will as the most important thing in your life. You serenely welcomed it at every moment, saying that one's own will is not pleasing to God; you lovingly held fast to God's plan even when that plan required that you die at the very fullness of your youth.

Help me to obtain the grace to live always according to God's plan for me. Teach me to accept the events that take place every day, even if unforeseen and painful, as an occasion for meeting God and for offering him my love.
Our Father; Hail Mary; Glory to the Father.

II.   Dear Saint Gabriel, I am deeply aware of the need for this grace: (*here, name the particular grace*). This will strengthen trust in God, increase Christian commitment, and help fulfill the aspirations of all. I hope that this request of mine is inspired by the Holy Spirit and a sign of the divine will.

Realizing that my prayer is weak and that my sinfulness prevents me from being heard, I turn to your intercession. Because of your love for the Crucified Lord and for Our Lady of Sorrows, you receive the many graces and miracles that you request from them; therefore obtain also for me the grace that I ask for.

Our Father; Hail Mary; Glory to the Father.

III.   Your earthly journey, O Saint Gabriel, was constant praise to God and witness to his love. You did not waste life's gifts, but fulfilled the Father's will and practiced Christian virtue to the point of achieving heroic sanctity.

Let me too, with the help of the grace that you will obtain for me, use my life to give glory to God. Teach me, according to your example, to bear witness to my Baptism by faithfully living the Christian life and serving my brothers and sisters according to the demands of my state of life.

Our Father; Hail Mary; Glory to the Father.

NOVENA
In Honor of Saint Gabriel

The following novena is used:
> *— to praise God for the glory he gave to Saint Gabriel;*
> *— to meditate on the example of Saint Gabriel and to take his example as a model for our own lives;*
> *— to give thanks;*
> *— etc.*

I.   Dear Saint Gabriel, your life in this world was lived without falling away from God. You experienced the love of your family, the joys of friendship, pain at the death of loved ones, the exhilaration of success: but you also found balance and the true meaning of things through your prayer and through living the Christian life.

Help us to place God at the center of our lives, and never to forget that everything that happens to us and around us is somehow connected to his will.

Our Father ...

II.   In your relationships with others, O Saint Gabriel, you were a source of joy for everyone and at the same you were able to bring your own aspirations to fulfillment. You were dutiful and loving with your parents, brothers and sisters, teachers, classmates, superiors and confreres, so much so that they virtually competed with each other to listen to you and to be with you.

May the Lord grant that we be open to others and attentive to their problems. Let us overcome our selfishness and the attitudes of domination that contaminate our various social relationships.

Hail Mary ...

III.   You loved the poor, O Saint Gabriel, and chose a life of poverty in the Passionist family. Ever since you were a little boy, you gave up certain foods and made an offering of your savings; as a Religious you looked after the needs of the poor and wrote your father telling him to be generous with them. May God grant that world leaders work for a more just distribution of goods.

Help us to renounce the hoarding of goods, for this is an injustice to the poor, and help us to share what we have with those who are most in need.

Glory to the Father ...

IV.   You were able to love people who were dear to you, and things in life that were beautiful, without falling into the trap of selfishness or claiming improper ownership. Your love was expressed in sincerity and purity, and in your life as a Passionist it was centered on Our Lady of Sorrows even while it was given to all of humanity whom you loved in Christ the Crucified Lord.

In our love, help us to look to the good of others rather than to our own good, and let us experience the theological virtue of charity, which is loving one another with the very love of God himself.

Our Father ...

V.   In the important decisions of your youth, O Saint Gabriel, you sought to find the will of God through prayer, advice, reflection and penance. You finally found your path when you accepted Mary's invitation to become a Religious.

May Mary our heavenly Mother watch over our journey so that, guided and protected by her mediation, we may make the choices that God asks of us and obtain fulfillment as Christians.

Hail Mary ...

VI.   You valued the good things of the world, O Saint Gabriel, but you did not accept any compromise with sin. After you made your profession as a Passionist, you were so guiltless that not even once did you consciously commit a venial sin.

Obtain for us the strength we need to overcome the dangers in our spiritual life and to faithfully receive the sacraments from which grace flows. Plead for us that we might receive from God's mercy the forgiveness we need.

Glory to the Father ...

VII.   Once you realized the importance of being in communion with God, you sought nothing but his will. You saw the events and people of your life as continuous messages of God and you wished to remove from your heart anything that was displeasing to him.

Help us too to understand that without God we are lost, whereas with faith in God, everything is given meaning and we are able to accept difficulties and also joy with greater authenticity.

Our Father ...

VIII.   It seemed that nothing could satisfy you, O Saint Gabriel, in your search for meaning and happiness. With the guidance of the Blessed Virgin, Our Lady of Sorrows, you discovered that Jesus, the Crucified Lord, is the fullness of everything and the culmination of love. From then on you wanted only to be conformed to him, giving your life in love to God and to humanity.

May the Crucified Lord help us to understand our lives as a vocation to be lived lovingly every day in the service that has been entrusted to us, even to the total giving of ourselves.

Hail Mary ...

IX. The day of your death, O Saint Gabriel, was the greatest day of your whole life. You had lived so totally immersed in communion with God that you waited only to move across the threshold of faith so that you could lose yourself in the eternal ecstasy of the vision of God.

As we work with the goods and values of this life, make us understand that they are not ultimate but only penultimate. God alone is the greatest good and the fullness that will satisfy every longing.

Glory to the Father ...

TRIDUUM
In the Form of a
Liturgy of the Word

FIRST DAY

Saint Gabriel Fully Accepts the Will of God

Introduction

Ever since he was a little boy, Gabriel had always been fascinated by the mystery of the will of God. In suffering the loss of his mother, of two brothers, and two sisters, he would hear his father Sante remind them that they had to accept "the adorable will of God." When he was not sure what way of life to choose as an adult, his teachers at the Jesuit school and his confessors would explain that every choice had to be made in obedience to the will of God, especially the fundamental choice of one's vocation in life. Once he had joined the Passionists, he came to see the will of God embodied in the community's Rule, in the service rendered by the Superiors, and in the different events that took place. He would be meticulous in his faithful observance of that will. He welcomed his studies, his prayer, the community, sickness and even death as the fulfillment of his own person, because this was God's will for him.

From the Word of God

This is how you are to pray: Our Father in heaven, hallowed be your name, your Kingdom come, your will be done, on earth as in heaven (Mt 6:9-10).

Then going out he went, as was his custom, to the Mount of Olives, and the disciples followed him. When he arrived at the place he said to them, "Pray that you may not undergo the test." After withdrawing about a stone's throw from them and kneeling, he prayed, saying, "Father, if you are willing, take this cup away from me; still, not my will but yours be done" (Lk 22:39-42).

While he was still speaking to the crowds, his mother and brothers appeared outside, wishing to speak with him. Someone told him, "Your mother and your brothers are standing outside, asking to speak with you." But he said in reply to the one who told him, "Who is my mother? Who are my brothers?" And stretching out his hand toward his disciples, he said, "Here are my mother and brothers. For whoever does the will of my heavenly Father is my brother, and sister, and mother" (Mt 12:46-50).

From the Writings of Saint Gabriel

You should rejoice rather than be saddened, dear father, if God has sent you some inconvenience or difficulty: for tribulations usually are the characteristic mark of those he has chosen. I know, dear father of mine, that your life has been like a wheel surrounded not so much by roses and happiness as by tribulations and thorns. Still, may the most holy will of Jesus and of Mary be done. One day you will reap the fruit of all this. (*Letter to his father, Pievetorina, February 1, 1859.*)

I do nothing but bless the merciful hands of the Virgin Mary who drew me from the world. Perhaps by this time I would already be a priest, if it were not for the lack of prelates to confer ordination, which has prevented me from progressing further. God has willed it so, and I too want it so. (*Letter to his father, Isola del Gran Sasso, December 19, 1861.*)

I will be punctual in my obedience, even leaving letters unfinished while I am writing. I will listen to the voice of my superiors and of the bells signalling the beginning of the various activities, as the voice of God. I will obey blindly without asking why, how or any other question. I will obey with my heart, intellect and judgment, being of one mind with whoever gave the orders, because for me all orders are ultimately from God. I will always say: I do this, O Lord, because it is what you want. (*Resolutions*, no. 30.)

Suggestion for Homily or Meditation

It is God's will that all human beings should attain happiness and complete self-fulfillment; that everyone should be free and equal, each giving of themselves for the good of others; that humanity and all of creation should be united and made whole in Christ. This is his plan of salvation and sanctification for all created realities.

In this plan, each person is called to play their own special and unique role, according to their personal vocation. A man or woman succeeds in life and finds self-fulfillment to the degree that they discover and take on the role that God has ordained for them.

This discovery is not easy, because it requires a journey of discernment that involves reading with eyes of faith the situations that one finds oneself in, listening to one's own conscience, praying and seeking advice.

Gabriel made this journey, encountering all the anxiousness that it entails, putting decisions off and hesitating in the face of the totality of self-giving that he nonetheless felt called to deep inside. But then he responded with generosity and gave his whole being in faithfulness to this call. Doing the will of God was the only thing that interested him. "One's own will is not pleasing to God, it just is not pleasing to him," he would say over and over. And facing death, his dream of becoming a missionary now over, he was serene and gave himself completely to the will of God. What did it matter if his most highly cherished project disappeared? The only thing that mattered was the will of God.

We are somewhat fearful of the will of God because we believe it may be contrary to our own will. But he desires that we be happy much more than we ourselves desire it. The problem is that his plan for achieving this happiness and our own plans for doing the same are often very different. The secret, then, is to try to be tuned in to the will of God; his will is never to be found in things that waste time or squander life.

Prayer

Recite a decade of the Rosary meditating on the first of the Joyful Mysteries (the Annunciation of Our Lord's Incarnation to Mary) *or the first of the Sorrowful Mysteries* (Our Lord's Agony in the Garden). *Or as an alternative, pray the following litany*:

Let us pray: God, Almighty Father, by the intercession of Saint Gabriel of Our Lady of Sorrows, grant that we may learn the fundamental prayer: your will be done.

— In times of joy and times of sadness,
    R. *Lord, your will be done.*

— In times of health and times of sickness,
    R. *Lord, your will be done.*

— In success and failure,
    R. *Lord, your will be done.*

— In the worries about our children's future,
    R. *Lord, your will be done.*

— In the problems of modern society,
    R. *Lord, your will be done.*

— In the uncertainties and the inability to see clearly when we are faced with choosing our path in life,
    R. *Lord, your will be done.*

— In the events that bring honor to humanity because they make men and women grow according to your plan,
    R. *Lord, your will be done.*

— In the evil that disgraces humanity, such as injustice, violence, drug abuse, pollution, things that we do not succeed in avoiding and that you mysteriously permit,
R. *Lord, your will be done.*

— In the situations that we do not understand but want to accept in a spirit of faith,
R. *Lord, your will be done.*

— When, despite efforts at dialogue, we do not understand each other,
R. *Lord, your will be done.*

— When, despite our commitment and every good intention, we are unable to avoid evil,
R. *Lord, your will be done.*

— In all circumstances of our life and at the hour of death,
R. *Lord, your will be done.*
Our Father ...

SECOND DAY

Saint Gabriel's Devotion
To Our Lady of Sorrows

Introduction

Gabriel saw in Our Lady of Sorrows a person who loved and who found self-fulfillment by giving of herself. During his childhood in Assisi and Spoleto, and throughout the period of his maturation to young adulthood, prayer and reflection with his family gathered around the statue of the Pietà gradually revealed to him that Mary was the person who faithfully stood by Jesus even up to his death on the Cross. Mary's sorrow was not frustration or sadness, but love that is close at hand and compassionate. Gabriel fell in love with Our Lady of Sorrows because he discovered in her a Christianity that was lived with utmost dedication to every person who was suffering.

From the Word of God

After they had completed its days, as they were returning, the boy Jesus remained behind in Jerusalem but his parents did not know it... After three days, they found him in the temple, sitting in the midst of the teachers, listening to them and asking them questions… When his parents saw him, they were astonished, and his mother said to him, "Son, why have you done this to us? Your father and I have been looking for you with great anxiety." And he said to them, "Why were you looking for me? Did you not know that I must be in my Father's house?" But they did not understand what he said to them. He went down with them and came to Nazareth, and was obedient to them; and his mother kept all these things in her heart (Lk 2:43, 46, 48-51).

Standing by the Cross of Jesus were his mother and his mother's sister, Mary the wife of Clopas, and Mary of Magdala. When Jesus saw his mother and the disciple there whom he loved, he said to his mother, "Woman, behold, your son." Then he said to the disciple, "Behold, your mother." And from that hour the disciple took her into his home (Jn 19:25-27).

From the Writings of Saint Gabriel

Are my brothers studying? Are they obedient? Are they showing a devotion to Mary, Our Most Blessed Lady of Sorrows, remembering always her sorrows, practicing constant devotion to her, especially in the recitation of the rosary? The mere thought of practicing constant devotion to this Mother of ours brings comfort in every misfortune, in every temptation, in every tribulation. Mary is the only ladder allowing us to climb to eternal happiness. I would be very grateful if you would take good care of my image of Our Lady of Sorrows, and if you would show it veneration in some way; this should be the memory you keep of me, it would be very pleasing to me and even more so to Mary Most Holy. (*Letter to his father, Morrovalle, May 23, 1857.*)

Dear father of mine, if only we trusted a little more in this tender Mother of ours! How much pain we cause her! She knows well the pains of childbirth with which she bore us on Calvary, when she accepted her dear Son's death on the Cross rather than witness the eternal damnation of our souls. If we would only think of this from time to time, perhaps then we would love even more our dear, tender Mother; we would trust her and would have no fear of hell. Rather, if we were tempted or threatened, or if we were frightened by damnation, our spirits would be raised by repeating: if Mary is with me, who could ever be against me? (*Letter to his father, Isola del Gran Sasso, December 27, 1860.*)

Suggestion for Homily or Meditation

Our Lady is sorrowful because she is the Mother of Christ, who died on the Cross in order to fulfill the Father's will: the salvation of humanity. In our modern language, "sorrowful" can have a negative connotation, but in this case its real meaning is one who loves, who is compassionate, who stands by others and remains with them even when the situation is incomprehensible or painful. The love with which one participates in these situations makes the experience of pain secondary.

For this reason, "Our Lady of Sorrows" is the title that best and most completely describes the spiritual mission and experience of Mary, from the Annunciation through Calvary up to her Assumption.

Gabriel grew up with a statue of the Pietà that was the predominant spiritual focus of the Possenti family. The dignity and strength of the Mother holding her dead Son in her arms left a lasting impression on him. His parents explained the meaning of the scene to him and the Holy Spirit guided him to a most profound understanding of that mystery.

He understood that the Crucified Lord and Our Lady of Sorrows represented love, love as the total response to the Father and love as the gift of life to humanity. He contemplated the Crucified Lord with the eyes and heart of Our Lady of Sorrows. He loved the Sorrowful Mother and drew from the love and tenderness that our Crucified Savior had for her. He felt that if he was to be conformed to the image of the Crucified Lord, he had to stand beside the Cross of Jesus, as his Sorrowful Mother had done; it was she who guided Gabriel's growth from childhood to the maturity to which he was called; it was she who was both model and mediatrix for him.

In the Church, Gabriel is a sign of Mary's mediation in the attainment of Christian holiness. With her example and her assistance in our lives we can come to understand God's will for us and to achieve the holiness that corresponds to our personal vocation.

Prayer

Let us pray to God the Father, asking that he give us the gift of his Spirit who will reveal to us the mystery of Jesus and the mystery of our sanctification in him.

R. *Through the intercession of Saint Gabriel, hear us O Lord.*

— For the Church: that it may be a community that listens to the Word of God and bears witness to his Word in life, so that, like Mary, it may make God present in history.

R. *Through the intercession of Saint Gabriel, hear us O Lord.*

— For the Pastors of the Christian community and the public leaders of society: that they may place themselves at the service of people, so that each nation and every individual will be able to take their proper place in God's plan.

R. *Through the intercession of Saint Gabriel, hear us O Lord.*

— For members of Religious Orders and for lay people: that each of them, according to their vocation, may bear witness to God's love in the world by a life lived for others.

R. *Through the intercession of Saint Gabriel, hear us O Lord.*

— For young people: that, called to married life or to Religious or priestly consecration, they may respond generously and work in Christ's name for the sanctification of history and of all created realities.

R. *Through the intercession of Saint Gabriel, hear us O Lord.*

— For parents and educators: that they may understand that guiding the personal growth of others is the task that is most similar to the act of creation; may they respect the plan of God and always be inspired by love.

R. *Through the intercession of Saint Gabriel, hear us O Lord.*

— For those who suffer in body or spirit: that the Holy Spirit may reveal to them the most precious gift that is theirs, for through their acceptance of pain they can give themselves to God and to others in union with the Crucified Christ.

R. *Through the intercession of Saint Gabriel, hear us O Lord.*

— For all human beings: that they may find the way of peace and unity, so that Christ's prayer and the purpose of his Death and Resurrection may find fulfillment.

R. *Through the intercession of Saint Gabriel, hear us O Lord.*

Father, hear our prayers. Grant us also the grace that we need even though we may not know that we need it. We ask you this through the love of Christ, your Crucified and Risen Son, through the faithful dedication of his Sorrowful Mother, and through the intercession of Saint Gabriel. You who live and reign for ever and ever.

R. *Amen.*

THIRD DAY

Saint Gabriel
Is Conformed to Christ Crucified

Introduction

Gabriel discovered the Crucified Lord in the arms of Our Lady of Sorrows. Just as the Cross is the summit of Mary's spiritual experience, so is the connection of Our Lady of Sorrows and the Crucified Lord the summit of Gabriel's spiritual maturity. The Crucified Lord is everything: all the love that can be given to God and to humanity; all the friendship, solidarity, forgiveness, understanding, dedication; he is the summation of all values, of every positive reality. Following the example of Our Lady of Sorrows, Gabriel came to model his life more and more after that of the Crucified Lord, consuming and fulfilling his own youthfulness in this undertaking.

From the Word of God

If anyone wishes to come after me, he must deny himself and take up his cross daily and follow me. For whoever wishes to save his life will lose it, but whoever loses his life for my sake will save it (Lk 9:23-24). Whoever does not carry his own cross and come after me cannot be my disciple (Lk 14:27).

For Christ... [sent me] to preach the Gospel, and not with the wisdom of human eloquence, so that the Cross of Christ might not be emptied of its meaning. The message of the Cross is foolishness to those who are perishing, but to us who are being saved it is the power of God (1 Cor 1:17-18).

May I never boast except in the Cross of our Lord Jesus Christ, through which the world has been crucified to me, and I to the world. From now on, let no one make trouble for me; for I bear the marks of Jesus on my body (Gal 6:14,17).

From the Writings of Saint Gabriel

Let us receive everything from the loving hand of God. Whoever does not carry the Cross of Jesus Christ and does not follow him cannot be his disciple. You will tell me that you are carrying the Cross; this is a good sign, for this is what the Lord wants of you. Afterward will come the time of consolation. (*Letter to his father, February 1860.*)

Jesus went to excess in order to show us his love. He could have saved us any number of ways — all it would have taken was a drop of blood, a tear, a prayer; it wasn't necessary that he die. But what would have been enough for justice was not sufficient for love. We deserved chains and ropes, and he wanted to be bound over in place of us; the insults and scourging should have been ours, and he underwent them for us; the sentence of condemnation was pronounced against us, but he accepted it in our stead. Lastly, the lot reserved for us was eternal death with the torments of hell, but he, in order to free us from this, chose to die in prolonged agony on a gallows without any relief.

I too was among the authors of your death, O Jesus! By my sin I put you to death, but I do not even want to think that you would deprive me of your forgiveness. Never! Your wounds call out to me, your arms invite me, your wounded heart offers me refuge. Here I am, then, in your presence, O Jesus Crucified! I ask for your mercy, I ask for your forgiveness. And you, O Mother of Sorrows, who had your beloved Son taken from you, do not permit that I also should be taken from you for ever, unworthy though I be, I am always your son. (*From a meditation on the Passion of the Lord, written by Saint Gabriel, perhaps in the year 1859.*)

Suggestion for Homily or Meditation

Being crucified means being in love with the Father and with all of humanity. Jesus did not die on the Cross because he had suffered a misfortune that he could not avoid, but because he loved the Father and wanted to do what the Father wanted. The Father wanted humanity to be saved, and Jesus worked to this end until his death.

Once he understood that this is the meaning of Jesus' death on the cross, Gabriel sought to imitate in his own life the dynamics of this love, with the mediation of Our Lady of Sorrows. He wanted to become a little version of him who was crucified. He willingly accepted the sacrifices of the Passionist life. To these he wished to add personal penances: he thought daily of Jesus' Passion; he studied diligently so that he could become a missionary and proclaim the love with which God loves every person in the Crucified Christ.

He was completely conformed to the Crucified Lord in a short amount of time. There was no need for him to become a priest or preacher in order to shout out to the world the love of Christ Crucified. A life lived as he had lived his was enough. The culminating of his life in death at twenty-four years of age was the final stage in the process of being conformed to Christ.

Loving God and humanity is the core of Christianity, the vocation and mission of every baptized person, regardless of the role they are called to play in the plan of salvation. The ultimate response is found in the Crucified Christ, a response that all of us are called to imitate. Gabriel shows us how to succeed in this.

Prayer

Dear Saint Gabriel, we thank you for the example of living that you have given us and that encourages us on our journey.

In your family's difficult moments and in your youthful wanderings you did not lose your balance but were able to distinguish God's call among the various choices that attracted you.

Help us also to overcome uncertainty, to open up closed doors, to give ourselves over to good by responding to the call of grace, to find meaning in this life that often leaves us baffled.

Thirsting for love and happiness like all of us, you understood that only in self-giving, to the point of relinquishing everything, could one truly receive and truly find, to the point of being able to satisfy every longing and desire. Our Lady of Sorrows showed you the Crucified Lord, and in the love of Christ and Our Lady you came to see the whole world and to find your own self-fulfillment.

We beseech you, let your example become a powerful intercession for us.

Obtain for us from the Lord the grace to

respond to our vocation with the same generosity and with the same good results that you had, according to our capacity.

Give us the certainty that we too can succeed, the hope that will allow us to go on even in the face of failure, and the interior joy of always being able to say that we did our best. Amen.

Our Father; Hail Mary; Glory to the Father.

The Echo of Saint Gabriel (*L'Eco di San Gabriele*) is a contemporary magazine featuring current events, culture and religion. It brings the message of Saint Gabriel to families and is an aid in understanding the facts and tendencies of the modern world in which we live. Regular columns and special features on Christian faith appear, and there are sections dealing with the important issues facing the world today and news items that are helpful for simple everyday living.

For further information, contact:

> L'Eco di San Gabriele
> 64048 S. Gabriele (TE)
> ITALY

The *Pious Union of Saint Gabriel* (*Pia Unione di San Gabriele*) is an association that gathers the friends of Saint Gabriel; together they commit themselves to imitating his example of living. A special Mass is celebrated for the associates of the Pious Union of Saint Gabriel the first Saturday of every month.

For further information, contact:

> Pia Unione di San Gabriele
> 64048 S. Gabriele (TE)
> ITALY